First Facts®

Expert Pet Care

CARING for Hamsters

by Tammy Gagne

raintree

a Capstone company — publishers for children

Raintree is an imprint of Capstone Global Library Limited, a company incorporated in England and Wales having its registered office at 264 Banbury Road, Oxford, OX2 7DY – Registered company number: 6695582

www.raintree.co.uk
myorders@raintree.co.uk

Edited by Marissa Kirkman
Designed by Sarah Bennett
Original illustrations © Capstone Global Library Limited 2019
Picture research by Tracy Cummins
Production by Laura Manthe
Originated by Capstone Global Library Ltd
Printed and bound in India

ISBN 978 1 4747 6089 8
22 21 20 19 18
10 9 8 7 6 5 4 3 2 1

British Library Cataloguing in Publication Data
A full catalogue record for this book is available from the British Library.

Acknowledgements
We would like to thank the following for permission to reproduce photographs: Alamy: Top-Pet-Pics, 17; Capstone Studio: Karon Dubke, 4, 5, 13; iStockphoto: Antagain, 14 Right; Shutterstock: AlexBukharov, 23, Allocricetulus, 21 Top, AtiwatPhotography, 19, ekmelica, Design Element, Elya Vatel, 3, fantom_rd, 20, Igor Kovalchuk, 14 Left, Jane September, 8, Kurashova, 21 Bottom, Lepas, 10, Natalia7, Back Cover, 24, Punyaphat Larpsomboon, 18, santypan, 15, Steve Design, 16, Viachaslau Kraskouski, Cover, Vicky du Toit, 7, Victor FlowerFly, 9, Vishnevskiy Vasily, 21 Middle, Weerawat Promchai, 11; SuperStock: Adrianko/ Cultura Limited, 6.

Contents

Your new pet hamster

Do you enjoy watching hamsters run around their cages? Hamsters make great first pets. You can buy these tiny animals at most pet shops.

Owning a hamster is a big **responsibility**. Before buying one, you should learn all about this **rodent**. Knowing how to care for a hamster will help you keep your pet happy and healthy.

FACT

There are different sizes and types of hamsters. You will need to choose a hamster that is right for you and your family.

responsibility duty or job

rodent mammal with long front teeth used for gnawing; rats, mice and squirrels are rodents

Things you will need

Your hamster will need a cage. A plastic cage with stainless steel bars at the sides is best. Give your hamster plenty of room to exercise.

Hamsters need **nesting materials** inside their cages. They also need an area of **litter** that is deep enough for them to **burrow** into. Your hamster needs a food dish, water bottle, exercise wheel, toys and a **nesting box**.

nesting materials materials used to make an animal's nest or bed; good quality hay or shredded paper can be used

litter area for hamsters to burrow; dust-free wood shavings can be used

burrow dig and hide

nesting box shelter where hamsters sleep and store food

Hamsters clean themselves in wood shavings. You can find these at your pet shop.

Bringing your hamster home

Give your hamster time to explore its new cage. Picking your hamster up too soon may scare it or cause it to bite. Start by placing your hand in the cage. Let the animal come to you and sniff your hand. Soon you will be able to pick it up safely. Be careful if you have larger pets. Dogs and cats can hurt hamsters.

Holding a treat can help get your hamster to come to you.

9

What do hamsters eat?

Feed your hamster **pellets** or seeds from the pet shop. This food is made with the **vitamins** hamsters need. Most hamsters eat at night. Keep fresh food and water in the cage at all times.

Hamsters also eat some types of fruit and vegetables. A tiny piece of apple or carrot is fine. Remove any food your pet doesn't eat the same day.

FACT

Never give your hamster onions, potatoes or oranges. These foods can make a hamster sick.

pellet small, hard piece of food; pellets give animals the nutrition they need

vitamin nutrient that helps keep people and animals healthy

Your hamster's cage

Make sure your hamster's cage is kept somewhere quiet. Do not put a hamster cage near a TV or computer as these make noise that can be stressful to hamsters.

Hamsters are **nocturnal** so make sure the cage is in a room where the lights are off at night.

Clean your hamster's cage once a week. Give your pet fresh bedding and nesting materials. Smell is important to hamsters, so keep some clean old bedding in the cage even after you have cleaned it. Wash and refill your pet's food dish and water bottle.

nocturnal active at night

Keeping your hamster healthy

Healthy hamsters have bright eyes and soft fur. A hamster that doesn't eat enough or sleeps too much may be sick.

If your hamster is unwell, take it to a **vet**. Make sure the vet treats small animals, including hamsters. Some vets only treat larger animals.

A hamster's hair may be long or short. Hamsters can be many colours such as black, brown or white.

vet doctor trained to take care of animals

Life with a hamster

Some small animals enjoy living in groups. But hamsters prefer to live alone. Keeping two or more hamsters in the same cage can lead to fights.

A hamster's front teeth never stop growing. Hamsters chew often to keep their teeth short. Give your pet plenty of toys to chew on.

Your hamster through the years

Hamsters usually live for about two to three years. Make sure your hamster has healthy food, lots of exercise and a clean cage. This will give your pet the best chance at a long life.

Hamsters can be very active at night. However, they become less active as they get older. They may sleep more and play a bit less.

Hamster body language

A hamster's **behaviour** says a lot about how it is feeling. When a hamster is tired, it folds its ear against its head. Picking it up at this time could cause it to bite. Hamsters stretch and squeak when they are happy. They may be more open to being held at this time. Always be careful and move slowly when holding your pet.

behaviour way a person or an animal behaves

Chinese hamster

Types of hamsters

The most common types of pet hamsters:

- Campbell dwarf hamsters
- Chinese hamsters
- Robo hamsters
- Russian dwarf hamsters
- Syrian hamsters (also called teddy bear hamsters)
- Winter white hamsters.

Russian dwarf hamster

Syrian hamster

Glossary

behaviour way a person or animal behaves

burrow dig and hide

litter area for hamsters to burrow; dust-free wood shavings can be used

nesting box shelter where hamsters sleep and store food

nesting materials materials used to make an animal's nest or bed; good quality hay or shredded paper can be used

nocturnal active at night

pellet small, hard piece of food; pellets give animals the nutrition they need

responsibility duty or job

rodent mammal with long front teeth used for gnawing; rats, mice and squirrels are rodents

vet doctor trained to take care of animals

vitamin nutrient that helps keep people and animals healthy

Find out more

Books

Care for Your Hamster (RSPCA Pet Guide), RSPCA (HarperCollins, 2015)

Looking After Hamsters (Pet Guides), Susan Meredith (Usborne, 2013)

Nibble's Guide to Caring for Your Hamster (Pets' Guides), Anita Ganeri (Raintree, 2014)

The Truth About Hamsters: What Hamsters Do When You're Not Looking (Pets Undercover!), Mary Colson (Raintree, 2018)

Websites

Find out more about pet care at:
www.dkfindout.com/uk/animals-and-nature/pet-care

Learn more about all sorts of animals and how to take care of them at:
young.rspca.org.uk/kids/animals

Comprehension questions

1. What sort of cage does your hamster need?

2. What jobs will you need to do to care for your pet hamster?

3. Name some foods that are harmful to hamsters.

Index